DATE DUE

J 793.7   June '05

Gibson

Learning Games

DEMCO

LEARNING GAMES

Ray Gibson

Illustrated by
Simone Abel, Lucy Su and Kim Blundell

Designed by
Lindy Dark and Non Figg

Edited by
Paula Borton

Series editors: Robyn Gee and Jenny Tyler

Contents

First published in 1993 by Usborne Publishing Ltd., Usborne House, 83-85 Saffron Hill, London, EC1N
8RT. England. First published in America August 1993. Copyright © 1993 Usborne Publishing Ltd.
The name Usborne and the devices ♀ ⊕ are Trade Marks of Usborne Publishing Ltd. All rights reserved.
No part of this publication may be reproduced, stored in any form or by any means, mechanical,
electronic, photocopying, recording or otherwise, without the prior permission of the publisher.
Printed in Portugal.
AE

READING GAMES

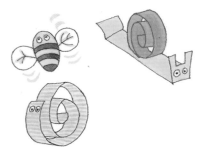

Parents and children can have hours of fun playing games with words and letters, and this book provides lots of ideas to introduce your child to the pleasures of reading. All the projects encourage the development of basic reading skills, while building up a general awareness of written and spoken language in everyday situations.

Getting ready for reading

Games are a great way to help children become readers. They provide a relaxed and informal learning situation in which a child is actively involved. In playing a game a child can see a limited number of words or letters lots of times, but not in a boring or repetitive way.

The games in this book will help your child learn to recognize letters and whole words, to realize that speech sounds are represented by letters and understand that words are made up of groups of letters. While helping make the things you need to play the games, your child will draw and paint letters and handle plastic magnetic alphabet shapes, becoming familiar with the names of all the letters. Make sure that the letters you write are always in lower case, except for proper names. Once your child has grasped the alphabet names, you could gradually introduce the sounds each letter makes. Don't rush this as it is easy to get confused, particularly when some letters make a variety of sounds: "g" in giraffe and "g" in gate makes a totally different sound in each case.

Make sure your child enjoys playing the games. Only play when she wants to and give lots of praise and encouragement.

Reading skills

Learning to read is a complex process which involves bringing together a lot of different skills. The ability to talk and listen with attention, to absorb and understand information, to concentrate and to observe and interpret pictorial information all play an important part. Children also need to know and experience the world around them and realize that they must bring this knowledge into their reading to support their understanding and enrich their imagination.

Sharing books

Games can help in the development of reading skills, but the best and simplest way to help develop them is to share books with a child. Games can then be a valuable supplement by building upon and reinforcing your child's knowledge and confidence.

Looking at, discussing, reading and enjoying books is the single most important thing that parents can do to encourage their children to become readers. Apart from the skills it develops, learning that books can be a source of pleasure, entertainment and information gives children a strong incentive for learning to read.

A good way to introduce children to books is to talk about the pictures. Choose scenes, such as the one below, that tell a story and are full of detail and action; this prepares children for reading stories in words.

Reading aloud

Reading aloud to children helps to expand their vocabulary and comprehension and to improve their listening and concentration skills.

It is now known that children who find it hard to recognize which words rhyme with each other find it difficult to learn to read. This sheds new light on the importance of sharing rhymes and poems with young children.

Stories can be an immense source of pleasure to children, even before they fully understand them. They quickly develop enthusiasms for particular stories and will want well-loved books to be read over and over again. When the story becomes very familiar to a child she will often start to join in,

a b c d e f g h i j k l m

Picture sequences are ideal for showing children how a story works.

especially with catchy, rhythmical phrases. She may like to pretend she's reading, holding the book and relating the story in her own words. She may also enjoy putting in her own sound effects, for instance in an animal story.

Discuss the story with your child. Drawing pictures inspired by a story is one way for a child to express what he has understood. Ask him to tell you about his picture and what is happening in it, also what happened just before and will happen just after, so he can get a sense of the order of events.

Looking at pictures

Children who have plenty of opportunity to look at pictures and talk about them, learn to "read" the pictures to find out what is going on in them. This is very useful when they first start to read, as clues from the pictures give them confidence to try the words underneath. When you look at picture books together, ask your child questions about the pictures and discuss what is happening. Play "find" games. Ask her what happened just before the action in the picture and what she thinks will happen next.

Learning how books work

A child who is used to using and sharing books will already have absorbed a lot of information that is needed before learning to read. She will understand, for instance, that you start at the front and work to the back and that you tackle each page from top to bottom and from left to right. Allow her to turn the pages for you to reinforce the front to back movement. Using a finger to trace underneath the words as you read them will help develop the top to bottom and left to right movements of reading.

Making up stories

Make up stories to tell your child, or make them up together, perhaps by asking questions. These have the advantage of being tailor-made to suit your child's particular interests. This will help develop your child's sense of what a story is.

Words all around you

Once your child has learned to enjoy stories, rhymes, jokes, tongue twisters and so on, you can then help him develop a general awareness of the written word and its usefulness in all sorts of everyday situations in which you use reading and writing to gain and impart information.

we went shopping

Learning to recognize and even write his own name is an important step. It helps establish the idea that groups of letters say the same thing to everyone who reads them. Write messages and labels for your child. You could also make books together about things you both enjoy, reinforcing the idea that reading and writing are closely linked.

Playing games with letters and words can be an enjoyable part of the gradual process of learning to read. Games such as making bingo cards, fishing with magnetic letters and making an alphabet wall hanging bring together both writing and reading activities, and are a pleasurable way for your child to come to grips with the world of books and print.

n o p q r s t u v w x y z

Alphabet fishing game

You will need:
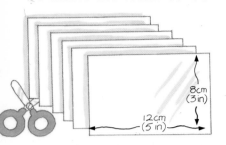 1 set of plastic magnetic letters in lower case

1 plastic straw for each player

strong thread

metal paper clips

rounded scissors

tape   ruler

To make the letter cards

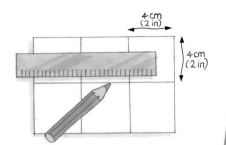

Cut strong white paper into six rectangles 12cm by 8cm (5in by 3in).

With a pencil, rule each piece into six squares.

4cm (2in)
4cm (2in)

Learning notes

This matching letters game will help your child become familiar with the names and shapes of the letters of the alphabet. Remember to say the letter names as they are fished.

Draw a large letter in pencil in each of the squares on the cards, using the ones here as a guide. Then go over the letters in thick felt-tip pen.

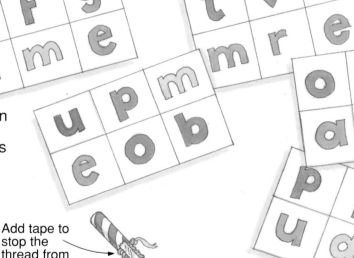

To make the rods

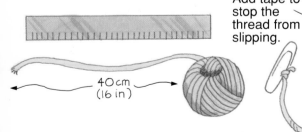

40cm (16 in)

Add tape to stop the thread from slipping.

Cut a piece of thread about 40cm (16in) long for each of the straws.

Knot one end to a metal paper clip and wind the other end around the straw, and then tie a knot.

Hints

•Draw the letters roughly the same size as the magnetic ones to make the matching easier.

•Number each card on the back to make sure you get a different one each time you play.

4

thick felt-tip pens

pencil

strong white paper

To play the game

Each player has one card and a fishing rod. Spread out the magnetic letters, placing them upside down.

Each player takes turns fishing for a letter. Players try to match their fished letters to the letter shapes on their cards. If the letter matches, it is placed over the drawn shape, otherwise it is put back. The first player to fill her card with plastic letters wins the game. Once children have mastered this game, they can play with up to three cards at once.

Other ideas

Once your child is familiar with lower case, you could try this game using capital letters, or a mixture of the two.

If you can't find magnetic capital letters, make your own by cutting them out of paper and taping on a metal paper clip.

Place them face down. Use a magnetic letter tied to a straw as a "fishing rod".

Messages

Put short simple messages on the refrigerator door for your child to read, such as "look under the bed". Leave a small "prize" for your child to find.

The lazy zookeeper

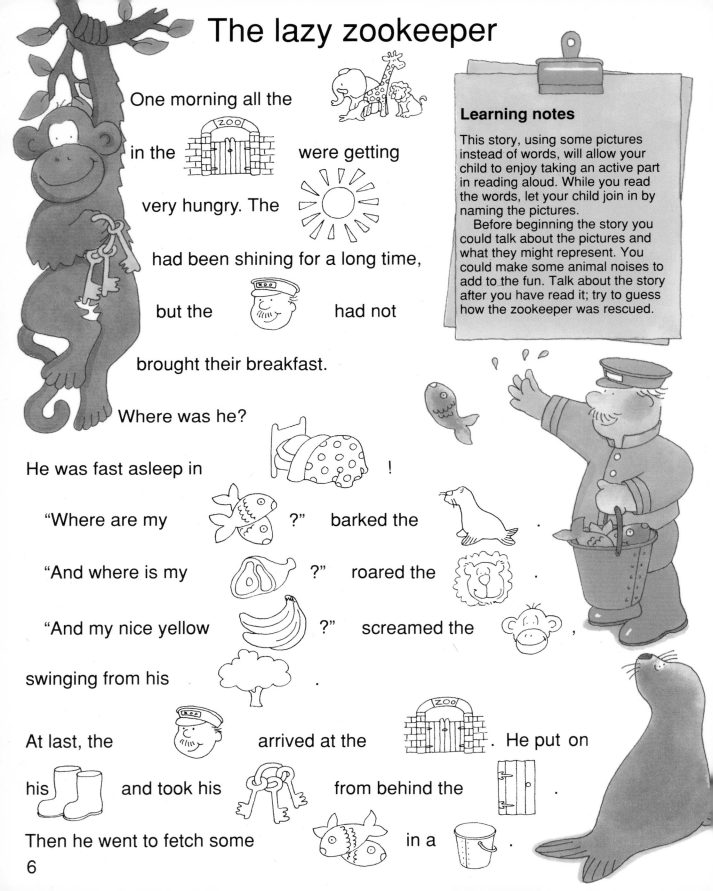

One morning all the [animals] in the [zoo] were getting very hungry. The [sun] had been shining for a long time, but the [zookeeper] had not brought their breakfast.

Where was he?

He was fast asleep in [bed]!

"Where are my [fish]?" barked the [seal].

"And where is my [meat]?" roared the [lion].

"And my nice yellow [bananas]?" screamed the [monkey], swinging from his [tree].

At last, the [zookeeper] arrived at the [zoo]. He put on his [boots] and took his [keys] from behind the [door]. Then he went to fetch some [fish] in a [bucket].

Of all the  the was the hungriest and the

angriest - and the naughtiest! He stole the  from the

keeper's coat and ran off to let the out!

"Where is our breakfast?" they cried, chasing the around

and around. He ran into an empty  and banged the

 behind him. Only a little white felt sorry for

him, and crept in through the to keep him company

until help arrived.

"I will have three  next to my bed from now on,"

said the , "so I will never be late again!"

And he never was.

Lily pond race

Learning notes

Coping with unfamiliar words can present problems, especially if they are not in context. Recognizing or "sounding out" the initial letter of a word can provide a powerful clue, and this game gives your child practice at this.

You will need:
green paper · rounded scissors · large paper bag · black felt-tip pen

start

To make the frog

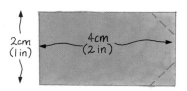

2cm (1in)
4cm (2in)

Cut a piece of green paper 4cm by 2cm (2in by 1in). Snip off the corners at one end.

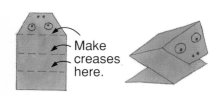

Make creases here.

Draw in the eyes and nose. Make three creases, as shown, then fold up the body so the frog sits up.

To make the caterpillar

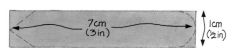

7cm (3in)
1cm (½in)

Cut another piece of green paper 7cm by 1cm (3in by ½in). Cut a pointed tail and a rounded head.

Fold the paper into a fan shape. Make sure the tail lies flat. Draw in the eyes.

To make the cards

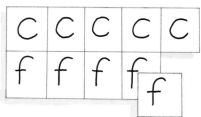

c c c c c
f f f f
f

Cut thin white cardboard into ten squares 2cm by 2cm (1in by 1in). Write "c" for caterpillar on five squares and "f" for frog on the rest.

ruler

thin white cardboard

To play the game

Put the cards in a paper bag and shake it. Each player takes turns to pick a card and name the letter. If it is a "c" the caterpillar moves one place closer to the pond. The frog moves if the letter "f" is turned up. The first to reach the lily pond is the winner.

Your child can also play this game by herself as it is the frog and caterpillar who are racing each other.

Other ideas

You can make other paper creatures to involve more first letter sounds. Make letter cards to match the first letter.

Snail

Tape on a paper "shell".

Moth

Cut the shape from folded paper.

W **Worm**

Curl up a strip of paper and tape it at the bottom. Draw in its eyes.

b **Bee**

Draw and cut out a paper bee.

9

Mice and cheese

To make each mouse

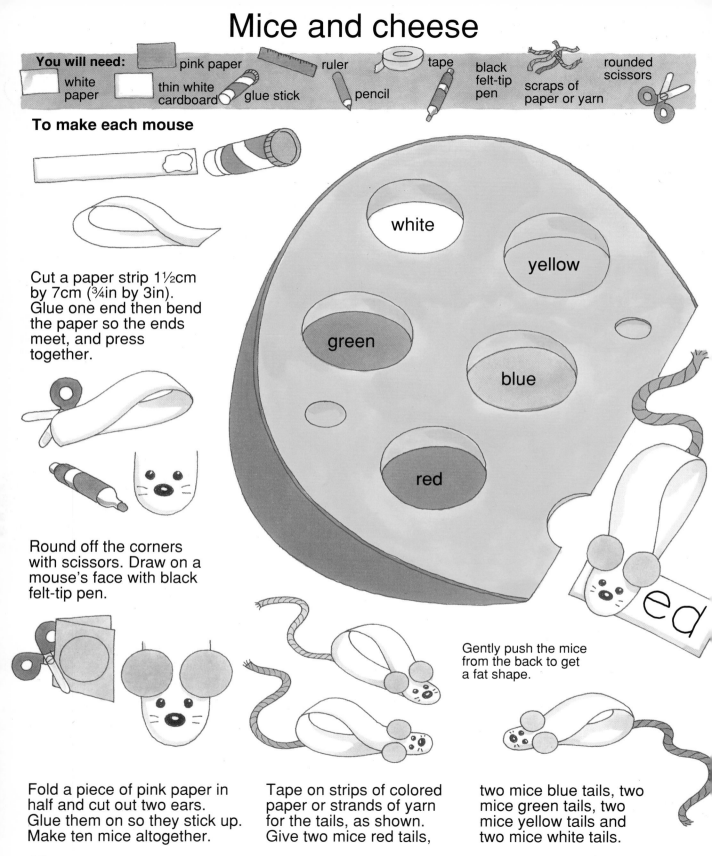

Cut a paper strip 1½cm by 7cm (¾in by 3in). Glue one end then bend the paper so the ends meet, and press together.

Round off the corners with scissors. Draw on a mouse's face with black felt-tip pen.

white
yellow
green
blue
red

Gently push the mice from the back to get a fat shape.

Fold a piece of pink paper in half and cut out two ears. Glue them on so they stick up. Make ten mice altogether.

Tape on strips of colored paper or strands of yarn for the tails, as shown. Give two mice red tails,

two mice blue tails, two mice green tails, two mice yellow tails and two mice white tails.

10

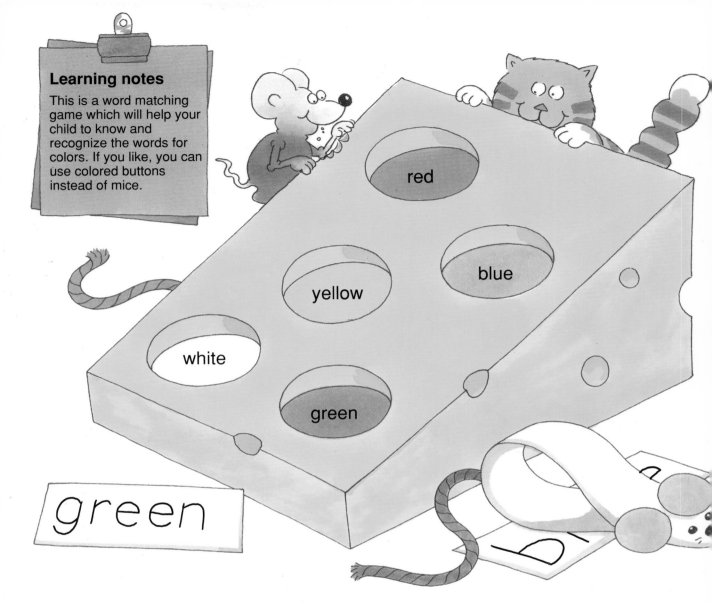

red

yellow

blue

white

green

To make the cards

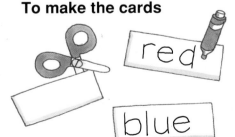

Make ten cards 6cm by 3cm (2½in by 1½in). Write "red", "blue", "white", "yellow" and "green" on pairs of cards.

To play the game

This is a game for two. Divide the mice so that both players have five mice, one of each color. The players each choose a cheese from this double page.

Spread the cards face down between the players who take turns picking up a card and reading the word. If the card, for example, says "red" the player can then put his red-tailed mouse on his cheese on the hole marked "red".

If the hole is already occupied, the card is put back. Move the cards around between turns. The first player to fill his own cheese wins.

Later on, you can cover the holes with paper circles marked with the names of other colors. Make mouse tails to match.

Time to go shopping

You will need: 1 set of plastic letters in lower case (you could use magnetic letters) paper bag

Hints

• You could use plastic capital letters at a later stage.

• If you pull an "x" out of the bag, look for word endings, such as "box". If this is too difficult take the letter out of the bag.

To play the game

Put the letters in a bag. The players pick a letter and name it. They then see what they can "buy" with it by finding an object beginning with that letter. You could put counters on objects that have been bought.

12

Other ideas

Using the picture only
Try playing I-Spy. One player chooses the first letter of an object in the picture while others guess what it is.

Using the letters and objects in your room
Place the letters around the room. The players have to see if they have been put in the right place, for example, they take off the letter "c" from the table and place it on the chair. You could put a time limit on this game to make it more exciting.

Using the picture and cards
On cards, write first and second letters of the objects which players have to guess, such as 'sn' for snake.

13

Spiders and drainpipes

You will need: 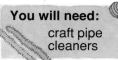 yarn 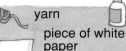 household glue rounded scissors thick paper

craft pipe cleaners piece of white paper glue spreader tape black felt-tip pen

To make the spiders

Cut a pipe cleaner in half and shape it into a ball. Tuck the sharp ends underneath.

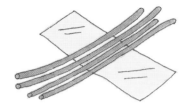

Cut four pieces of yarn about 10cm (4in) long. Lay them close together on a strip of tape.

Press the ball firmly onto the tape so that it sticks. Now trim the tape on either side.

Trim the legs so they are even on both sides, about 3cm (1in) long.

Cut small eyes out of white paper. Glue them on and draw in the pupils with felt-tip pen. Make one spider for each player.

To make the cards

Cut 8 pieces of thick paper 4cm by 6cm (1½in by 2½in). Clearly write "up" on four of the pieces and "down" on each of the remaining cards.

Learning notes

This game will help your child learn to sight read simple words. Once "up" and "down" have become familiar you can introduce three "stop" cards to the pile. When a "stop" card is turned up, the spider must then stay where it is for that "turn". At a later stage you can make cards that read "go forward one" and "go back one". This can be developed to "go forward two", "go back two" and so on up to four. Remember to introduce only one number at a time.

Playing spiders and drainpipes

The object of this game is to see which spider can reach the web first.

Mix the "up" and "down" cards and place them in a pile in front of the players.

To start, place the spiders on the rain barrel at the bottom.

The first player throws the dice. The spider is then moved along the spaces according to the number shown on the dice. The next player has a turn and the game continues.

If a spider lands on the brick squares where two drainpipes meet, the player must pick up the top card on the pile and read the instruction. If it is an "up" card the spider must go up the drainpipe and if a "down" card is turned up, the spider is moved down. The card is then returned to the bottom of the pile.

14

To play the game you will need: One spider for each player. dice 8 cards

Hint
Instead of making "pipe cleaner" spiders, each player can draw a spider on a square of strong paper.

15

Bingo

You will need:

stiff colored paper

stiff white paper

thick black felt-tip pen

paper bag

rounded scissors

1 set of plastic letters

Cut stiff white paper into four rectangles 20cm by 10cm (8in by 4in). Draw eight squares onto each piece.

Cut out small pictures from magazines, not more than 5cm by 5cm (2in by 2in). Choose pictures so that you get a good mix of first letters.

Glue a picture onto each of the white spaces on the cards.

Put the cards aside to dry. In the meantime you can make the counters.

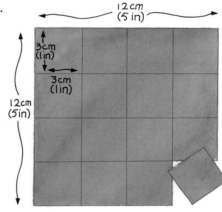

Cut a square of colored paper 12cm by 12cm (5in by 5in). Then divide it into squares 3cm by 3cm (1in by 1in). Cut them out to make paper counters.

Hints

- If there are more than two players you will have to make more paper counters.

- You can be flexible when naming the pictures: "carrot" can also be "vegetable"; "rabbit" can also be "animal".

- Talk about the pictures as you cut and glue them. Emphasize the sound of the first letter as you say the words.

16

old catalogs
and magazines

pencil

ruler household
glue

glue
spreader

Learning notes

Besides having a lot of fun playing this game, your child will learn to recognize letters and the sounds they represent. It will also help develop listening skills and concentration.

To play the game

Put the plastic letters in a paper bag. Remove any extra letters so that you just have the 26 letters of the alphabet.

Each player has a white picture card and eight paper counters. Players take turns pulling a plastic letter out of the bag and saying its name. Whoever has a picture starting with that letter, places a counter over that square on his card. The letter is then returned to the bag. The first player to cover his card is the winner. Swap the cards around for each game.

Other ideas

Word bingo

At a later stage you can make this into a word-reading game. Make word cards to match the pictures. Place them in a pile face down and see if you can match the words with the pictures as they are turned over. The cards are placed over the pictures instead of counters.

carrot

bee

house

hat

ring

Color bingo

Play color bingo by making cards with only six spaces. Color each square differently. Write the names of the colors on small squares and put them in a bag. Players play color bingo by matching the words with the colors.

red

ye

pink

green

blue

Country garden

ball

cake

gate

table

dog

flower

spade

bird

To make the cards and counters

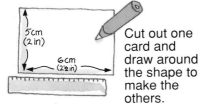

5cm (2 in)

6cm (2½ in)

Cut out one card and draw around the shape to make the others.

Using a pencil and ruler, cut 20 cards measuring 6cm by 5cm (2½in by 2in) out of thin white cardboard.

cake

fish

tree

On each of 16 cards write one of the words from the picture. On the remaining four cards draw a balloon. These four are your jokers.

Cut 16 counters about 2cm by 3cm (1in by 1½in) from colored paper.

18

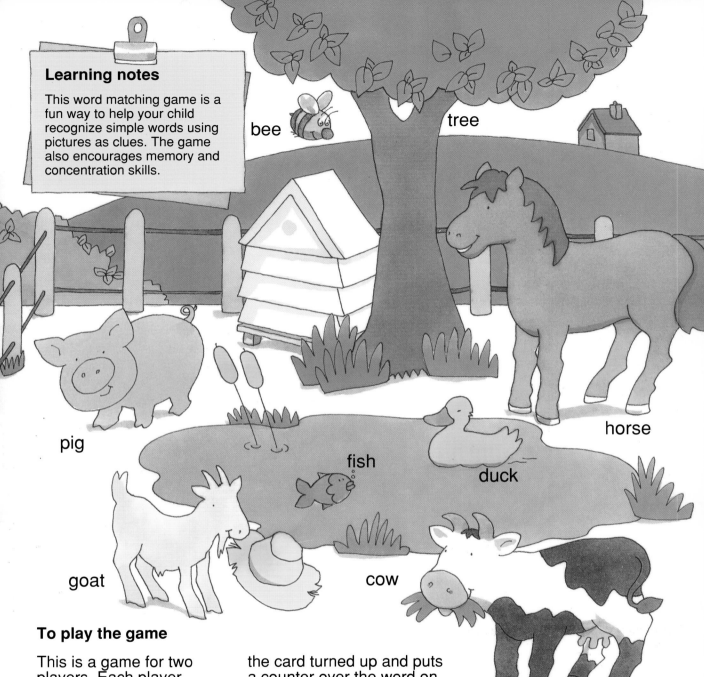

bee

tree

horse

pig

fish

duck

goat

cow

To play the game

This is a game for two players. Each player chooses one side of the double page - the field or the garden.

Lay the word cards in rows face down between the players. One person turns up a card and reads the word. If he can match that word to a word on his side of the page he leaves the card turned up and puts a counter over the word on the page. He turns the card back over if he cannot match the word. The other player then has a turn and so on. If a joker card is turned up the player misses a turn. Joker cards are left turned up. The first player to cover all the words on his side of the page is the winner.

Other ideas

Use the scene here as a "talkabout" picture or to play I-Spy. See if you can make up a story about the picture.

I can

You will need:

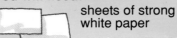

sheets of strong white paper

sheet of colored paper

black felt-tip pen

To make the word cards and paper counters

Cut some strong white paper to make 30 cards about 8cm by 4cm (3in by 2in) each.

With a pencil, clearly write all the words from this double page onto the cards, one word per card. Then go over the letters in black.

Now cut 30 squares from colored paper about 2cm by 2cm (1in by 1in). These are your counters.

I can

run

paint

eat

dance

swim

cook

blow

talk

drink

count

wash

drive

20

pencil

ruler

rounded scissors

Hint
Use an envelope to store the words and counters.

fly

kick

cry

read

skate

jump

smell

sleep

brush

hide

stretch

dig

To play the game

This is a game for two.

One player decides to be Mouse, and the other player is Cat. Now divide the word cards into two piles, face down, one for Cat and one for Mouse.

The first player then turns over a card from her pile saying "I CAN" and tries reading the word. She can use the pictures and words on the page to help. Whoever has that word on his or her side of the page then covers that word with a paper counter.

The second player now takes a turn and the game continues until one side is covered with counters. The first player to cover his side is the winner.

Other games to play

Match-its

Spread out all the word cards face down. Players take turns calling out a word on the page. The word caller then has to find and claim the word by turning over three cards. The player with most cards wins.

Miming game

This game just uses the cards and needs at least three players. Place the cards face up. A player mimes one of the actions. The others try to be the first to pick the right word card to fit the action.

Eggs on a plate

You will need:
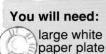
large white paper plate
brass paper fastener
ballpoint pen
ruler
thin cardboard
rounded scissors
felt-tip pens
red paint
paintbrush

To make the spinner

Widen holes if the pointer does not spin.

Turn over a large paper plate and divide it into six sections. Write "egg on" and "egg off" in alternate spaces around the rim.

Cut a piece of thin cardboard 10cm by 2cm (4in by 1in) and trim one end to a point. Paint it red and let it dry.

Use a ballpoint pen to poke a hole in the middle of the plate. Poke another hole in the pointer 1cm (½in) from its straight edge.

Push a paper fastener through the pointer and the middle of the plate and then open its wings. Make sure the pointer spins smoothly.

To make the eggs

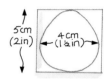

Cut a piece of thin cardboard 4cm by 5cm (1½in by 2in). Draw an egg shape and cut it out. Make 12 of these and decorate them like Easter eggs.

Hints

- Draw and cut out one egg and use the shape to draw the others.

- Instead of decorating the eggs, you could cut six from white paper and six from brown.

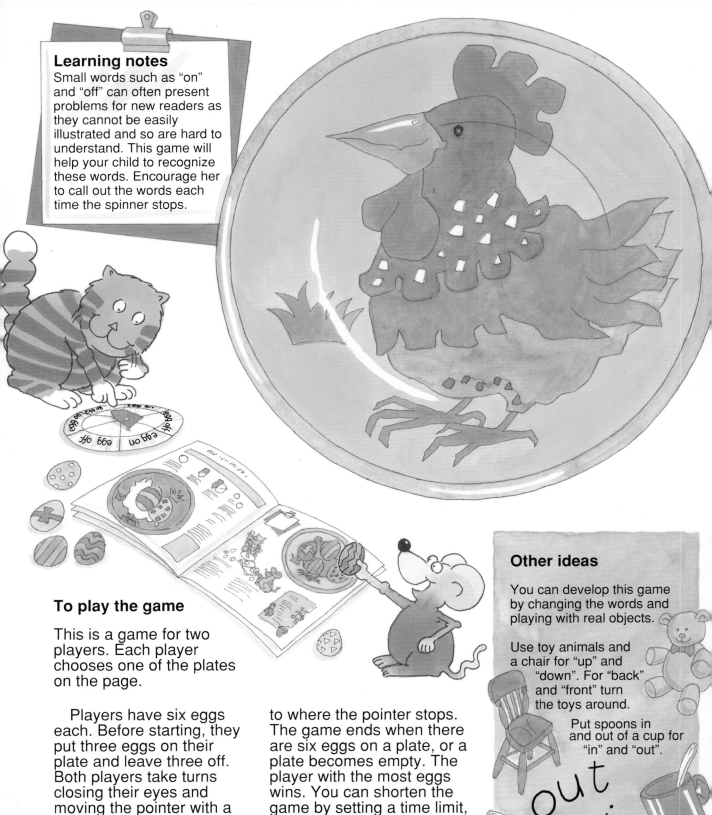

Learning notes

Small words such as "on" and "off" can often present problems for new readers as they cannot be easily illustrated and so are hard to understand. This game will help your child to recognize these words. Encourage her to call out the words each time the spinner stops.

To play the game

This is a game for two players. Each player chooses one of the plates on the page.

Players have six eggs each. Before starting, they put three eggs on their plate and leave three off. Both players take turns closing their eyes and moving the pointer with a finger. An egg is moved on or off their plates according to where the pointer stops. The game ends when there are six eggs on a plate, or a plate becomes empty. The player with the most eggs wins. You can shorten the game by setting a time limit, or reducing the number of eggs needed to win.

Other ideas

You can develop this game by changing the words and playing with real objects.

Use toy animals and a chair for "up" and "down". For "back" and "front" turn the toys around.

Put spoons in and out of a cup for "in" and "out".

23

Alphabet wall hanging

To make the wall hanging

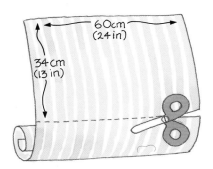

Cut a piece of wallpaper 34cm (13in) by 60cm (24in). This is the backing panel for the wall hanging.

Fold back the flap of a small envelope. Place the envelope so it is close to the long edge of the wallpaper.

Learning notes

This wall hanging will help famliarize your child with the letters of the alphabet. Once your child learns to recognize letters and know the sounds they represent, he will have a valuable key to reading.

Don't be in a hurry to teach alphabetical order, although you may be surprised at how quickly children learn it, especially if it is sung.

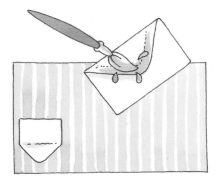

Wet the glued strip on the envelope's flap and stick it onto the wallpaper as shown.

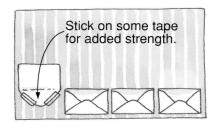

Stick on some tape for added strength.

Fold the envelope back down over its flap. Stick on three more in the same way.

To make the letters

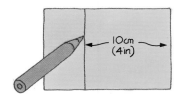

Cut four rectangles of wallpaper, 15cm by 10cm (6in by 4in). Draw a line on each piece 10cm (4in) from the short edge.

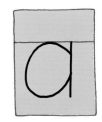

Turn the paper upside down to draw letters with tails.

In pencil, draw a letter in the space under your drawn line.

Treasure hunt

Scatter pictures around the house. The first player to place three pictures in the correct envelopes is the winner.

If there is only one player see how many pictures can be found to place in the right envelopes.

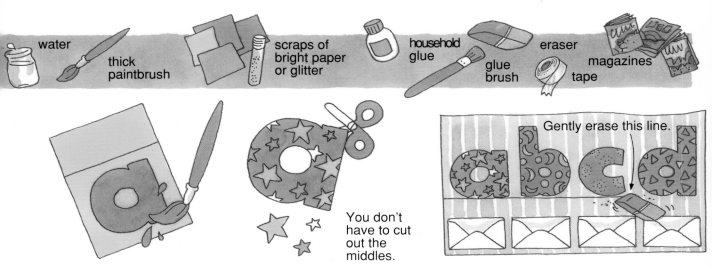

water

thick paintbrush

scraps of bright paper or glitter

household glue

glue brush

eraser

tape

magazines

Gently erase this line.

You don't have to cut out the middles.

Paint over the pencil letter with a thick paintbrush. Let the paint dry.

Now cut around the letters and then decorate them by gluing on small pieces of bright paper and glitter. Let the glue dry.

Draw a pencil line on the wallpaper 7cm (3in) from the top of the envelopes. Then glue on the letters, using the line as a guide.

Place the wall hanging within easy reach.

You can cut out lots of letters from magazines and glue them onto the envelopes. You can stick on capital letters as well.

Collect pictures from catalogs or magazines to put into the envelopes. A picture of a cat is put into the "c" envelope and so on.

As your child's knowledge grows you can make more wall hangings, continuing until you have completed the whole alphabet. For older children make a different wall hanging with capital letters.

25

I went to the circus

boots

cup

ball

horse

hat

To play the game

This is a game for two players, although if you have counters in more than two colors you can include other players.

The first player takes a letter out of the bag and says "I went to the circus and I saw..", then tries to find something in the picture beginning with that letter. The labels on the page can be used as a guide. There are plenty of things to spot here: from simple names such as "dog" to more complicated doing words such as "galloping". When something is found, the player then puts her color counter in the cup. The letters are returned to the bag. The game ends after an agreed time, say, ten minutes. The winner has the most counters in the cup.

26

swinging

Learning notes

This is an excellent way to expand your child's vocabulary and develop her observational skills. The game is open-ended and your child can progress from spotting simple words such as "dog" and "ball" to more complex words such as "swinging", "splashing" or "juggling".

water

shoes

pie

feet

drum

balloon

wag

27

Candy jar

You will need: scraps of bright paper or foil   rounded scissors   black felt-tip pen

To make the counters

Cut 12 candy shapes, as shown, out of scraps of paper or foil. These are your counters.

To make the cards

Make a small mark below letters to show the right way up.

Cut 22 white cards 3cm by 3cm (1½in by 1½in). On each of 21 cards write a letter of the alphabet, leaving out the vowels. Draw a candy cane on the remaining card. This is your joker.

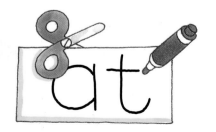

Cut a large card 8cm by 3cm (3in by 1½in). Write the letters "at".

To play the game

This is a game for two players. Before starting, each player chooses one of the candy jars on the page.

Place the card which reads "at" face up. The smaller cards are dealt out, face down, between the players. Players take turns picking up and placing one of their cards in front of the "at" card to try and make a word. If a player makes a word she can place a counter in her jar. The joker card, when turned up, can stand for any letter. The game ends when all the letters are used. The candies are then added up.

28

thin white cardboard

ruler

Learning notes
This game will help your child recognize that the same groups of letters can occur again and again in making up different words. Tackling groups of letters does not have to be a big step for your child even though she will be learning to link vowel sounds with consonants. Sound the letter and the word endings clearly and then let your child try to join them together. A lot of patience will be needed at first, especially as there are no pictures to help.
Remember to explain the meanings of words she may not know.

c at

Hints
• You could collect shiny chocolate wrappers and play this game with real jars. If you don't want to make the counters use buttons or plastic counters.

• To shorten the game you could agree that the first player who puts six candies in the jar is the winner.

Silly sentences

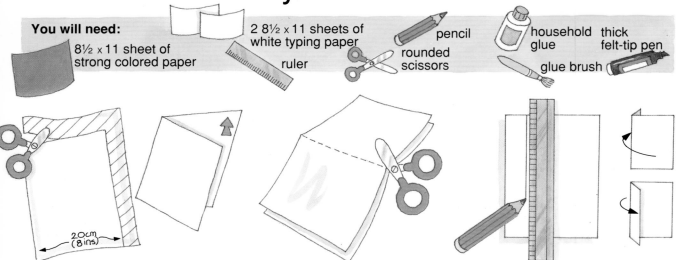

You will need:

8½ x 11 sheet of strong colored paper

2 8½ x 11 sheets of white typing paper

ruler

rounded scissors

pencil

household glue

glue brush

thick felt-tip pen

Trim both pieces of white paper so that they measure 28cm by 20cm (11in by 8in). Then fold them so that the short edges meet.

Open the folded sheets and then cut along the middle creases so that you have four separate pieces.

Draw a line on each piece 2cm (1in) from the left-hand long edge. Fold the paper back and then forward along these lines.

Learning notes

This is a fun way to introduce your child to recognizing whole sentences. This is not necessarily a huge step from dealing with individual letters and words, especially if you include words in the flip book with which your child is already familiar.

Other ideas

You can make up sentences about your family and friends, such as "Dad snores in bed" or "Anna walks to school".

Try changing the sentences in your book by gluing a fresh piece of paper on top of the old word strips.

Draw lines down the pages, leaving a 4cm (2in) gap between each line. You should have four spaces.

Then write a sentence along each page with a thick felt-tip pen.

Cut through all
four pieces.

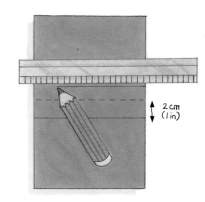

2cm
(1in)

Spread a little glue on the
margin of one of the pages
and then press another page
on top. Repeat this until all
the pages are stuck together.

When the glue is dry, cut
along your four drawn lines
to the margin.

Fold your colored paper so
the short edges meet. Open
it and draw a line 2cm (1in)
from the fold on either side.

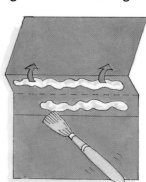

Fold the top page back along
the drawn line to make a
crease. Open it again and
spread glue between the
drawn lines.

we wash your cakes

Place the book along the
middle crease. Then close
the cover and press hard
along the glued area.
Let it dry.

Flip over the sections in
your book to read the silly
sentences.

Hint

Spread the glue thinly to keep
the paper from wrinkling.

Materials and equipment

Many of the games in this book involve making things. This is part of the fun so let your child join in such activities as drawing, cutting out and gluing. Talk about the things you are making but try not to make the games sound too complicated: most children will pick up games as you play them. You might want to make the pieces in one play session and play the game in another. You can cover any cards you make with sticky-backed plastic to protect them. Store them in an envelope for safekeeping.

The specific things you need for each project are listed at the top of each page. Below is some general advice on materials and equipment.

Paper: It is a good idea to keep a box where odd scraps of paper can be collected. This could include large, used envelopes; thin cardboard cut from cereal boxes and such things as shiny wrappers, colored foil and cellophane. Save old newspapers as you will need these to spread over your work surface, if you are painting or gluing. Magazines make a good source for cut-out pictures and lettering. Rolls of unused wallpaper are excellent for making cards, counters or book covers.

Felt-tip pens should be nontoxic and washable. Try to have both thick and thin pens. For early readers, lettering in black pen on white paper is very clear and easy to read.

Paints: Remember to buy only water-based paints. Ready-mix paints are sold in large stationery stores and stores selling educational toys. You can also use poster paints for small areas. Mix or thin the paints on old plates, and use old mugs for water as they are less easily knocked over than jars. Thick paintbrushes are easier to handle than thin ones. Don't forget to protect all your working surfaces with newspaper.

Scissors should be rounded. If you use sharp scissors remember to put them away immediately after use. If you have to cut out pictures of objects, draw a simple shape around the item so your child can see where to cut.

Glue: household glue is white but is clear when dry. It can also be used as a varnish or mixed with paint to act as a thickener. Although it does wash out of clothes, it is best to wear aprons or overalls while using it. Wash your brushes immediately after use. You can buy household glue in all large stationery stores and stores selling educational toys. Glue sticks are clean and easy to use and are good for sticking small areas. Do not use solvent based glues.

Adhesive tape: Cut all the pieces you need and stick them on a surface ready to use.

Plastic letters are often magnetic and invaluable for many word games. It is good to have two sets as you can then make words and sentences without running out of often-used letters. Try and get both small letters and capitals if possible, although be careful not to mix them at an early stage as this can confuse young children.

Pipe cleaners are sold in craft shops and educational toy stores and come in a great variety. You can also paint ordinary pipe cleaners.

Paper clips: Brass "wing" paper fasteners can be bought in office supply stores. It is a good idea to keep flat paper clips linked together and make sure all such small objects are out of the reach of very young children.

Paper bags are much safer than plastic ones. Discourage children from putting any kind of bag on their heads - they may not remember which is safe.

YOU AND YOUR CHILD
NUMBER GAMES

These number games can be played using cards, dice
and counters. All the games offer hours of entertainment
while, at the same time, enabling your child to recognize
numerals from one to ten and develop a general
understanding of numbers.

Learning about numbers

Games are an ideal way to introduce your child to early number skills. Most children need repeated practice with numbers in order to master these skills, and, in this book, the games to play on the opened pages offer a relaxed context in which to do this. Children who have fun and enjoy their first encounters with numbers will be much more likely to develop a positive, confident attitude toward math.

Early number skills

Young children are aware of numbers from a very early age and there are many ways to build on this. Number rhymes and songs are an amusing way of familiarizing small children with the names of number symbols. Making and looking at patterns is also an entertaining and useful exercise, preparing children for number patterns at a later stage.

Even such everyday activities as sorting things into groups, is an essential part of learning to count. By differentiating between various objects, children will start to think about sameness and difference and how things can be categorized. Let your child do such jobs as sorting out the cutlery after washing the dishes or sorting out the washing into piles.

Help your child become aware of the importance of numbers in everyday life. While on an outing you could count the number of red cars that go past or read the individual numerals on buses, house doors and so on.

Developing the power of estimation is also a useful skill. Ask your child to guess how many oranges there are in a bag, for instance, then count them out together. Remember to keep all your comments positive to build up confidence.

Number games

Many children can recite numbers at a very early age. This is not the same as being able to count, as they also need to be able to match number words to objects.

When playing number games, children can have fun while starting to learn that number words represent a corresponding number of objects. Many of the games in this book are designed to help children to recognize the numerals up to ten, to name them and to understand what they represent.

Another basic concept that children need to grasp is that the number of objects in a group does not change when they are arranged in different ways. This is known as "conservation of number" and your child can be introduced to this by playing Count the spots on page 38 and Jungle safari on page 54. Knowing where a number comes in relation to other numbers is also a useful skill and children can have a practice at this in Spiders go home on page 48 and also in Cups and saucers on page 44.

Becoming familiar with ordinal numbers, first second, third and so on, enables children to know where things come in order. By racing teddy bears (page 50) children will have a good introduction to these numbers.

Making the games

Before you start some of the games, you will need to make a few items. This is a valuable activity in itself and will afford opportunities for talking about numbers.

If your child's pencil control is fairly good, you could draw any numbers needed in pencil, for your child to trace over in felt-tip pen. This is good practice for learning to write numbers at a later stage.

Allow your child to help you use a ruler when you are measuring. Explain what you are doing and let her try to find the numbers you need and mark the right place with a pencil.

Playing the games

Most of the games are played on the opened pages of the book, using dice, counters or cards. While playing the games, encourage your child to do your counting as well as her own. Count out loud together slowly and deliberately.

If items have to be counted up at the end of the game, line them up in rows and see which one is the longest. Then count them out together.

When using plastic numbers, it is a good idea to place them on a piece of plain paper where they can be clearly seen, and will relate more easily to a written number.

If your child finds it difficult to pick up a single card from a pile, spread them out face down on the floor instead, to be picked up at random.

Give children all the help and support they need to create a relaxed atmosphere.

Having fun

You can work through this book from beginning to end or dip into it at random, bearing in mind that the simpler games come at the beginning. However you choose to use it, the emphasis should always be on having fun. If your child finds a game which she enjoys and wants to play again and again, she will be reinforcing the skills she has acquired. If she becomes bored or tired before a game is finished, stop the game or change the activity to shorten it.

Children learn at very different rates and have different attention spans. The most effective way to help your child is to be guided by her natural attention span and to recognize her individual learning pace.

Candles on the cake

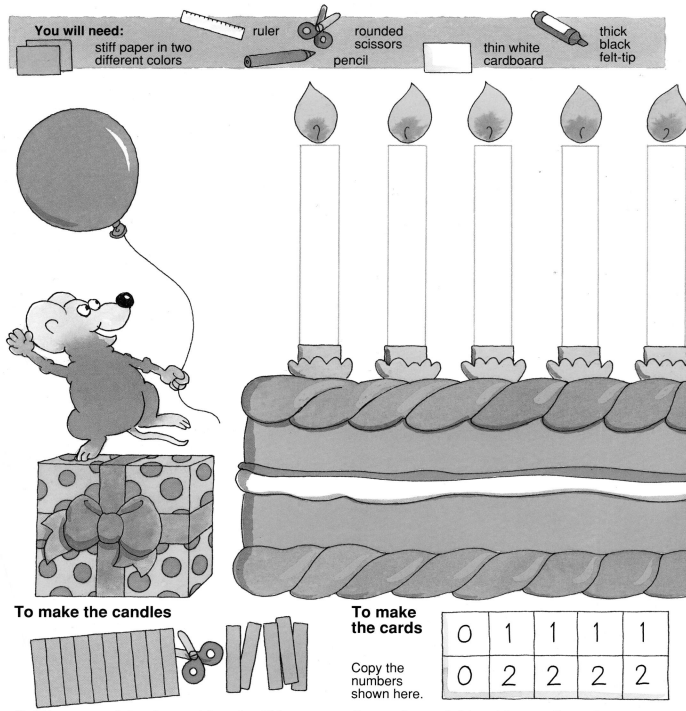

You will need:
stiff paper in two different colors
ruler
rounded scissors
pencil
thin white cardboard
thick black felt-tip

To make the candles

Cut the paper into pieces 10cm by 5½cm (4in by 2in). Using a pencil and ruler, divide the pieces into strips 5½cm (2in) long and 1cm (½in) wide. Now cut them into "candles".

To make the cards

Copy the numbers shown here.

0	1	1	1	1
0	2	2	2	2

Cut a piece of thin white cardboard to measure 20cm by 10cm (8in by 4in). Then using a pencil and ruler, divide it into ten rectangles. Clearly mark the numbers with felt-tip pen in the spaces and then cut along the lines to make ten cards.

To play the game

This is a game for two. Shuffle the cards and place them face down. Each player, in turn, takes a card and puts candles on the cake above, according to the number marked - "0","1" or "2". You must have an exact number to fill the last spaces.

The game is over when all the spaces for the candles have been filled. Take off all the candles and lay them in two lines according to color. Whoever has the longest row is the winner.

Other ideas

For very young children, draw candles on the cards so they can match the number of candles to be put on the cake with those on their card. Leave the "0" cards blank.

You could introduce a "taking away" exercise by placing on the cake an equal number of candles of each color. Players take away candles according to the number shown on the cards; an exact number must be turned up at the end. The winner is the first to take off all his candles.

Count the spots

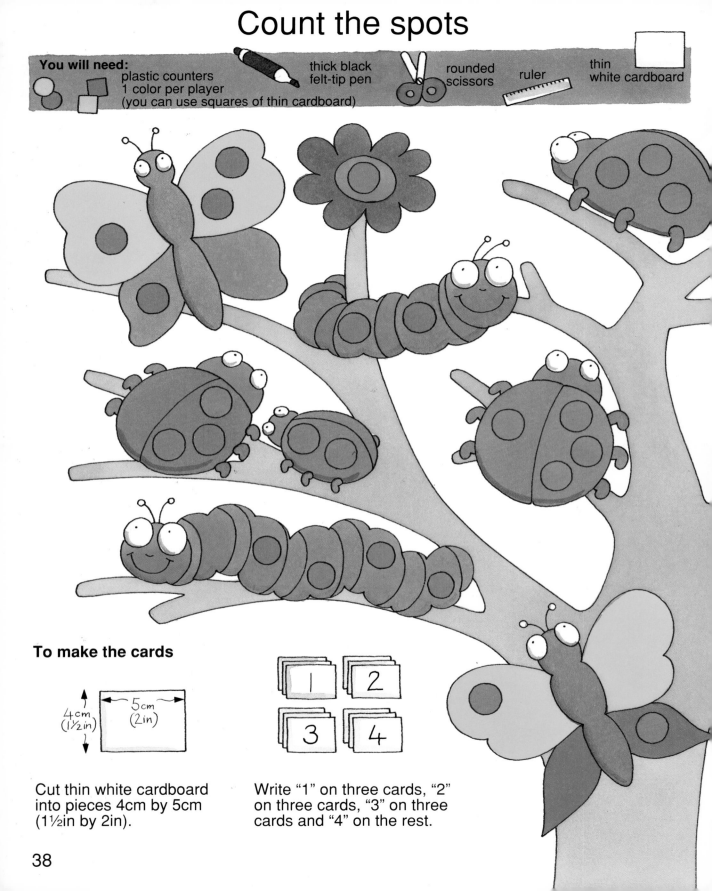

You will need:
plastic counters
1 color per player
(you can use squares of thin cardboard)
thick black felt-tip pen
rounded scissors
ruler
thin white cardboard

To make the cards

4cm (1½in)
5cm (2in)

1 2
3 4

Cut thin white cardboard into pieces 4cm by 5cm (1½in by 2in).

Write "1" on three cards, "2" on three cards, "3" on three cards and "4" on the rest.

38

To play the game

This is for two to three players. Each player has 10 counters.

Shuffle the cards and place them face down between the players. The players take turns in taking a card and then, according to the number shown, putting a counter on the creature or flower with the same number of spots. Cards are put back under the pile. If a player cannot find a number to match, she misses a turn.

The game ends when all the creatures and flowers on the page are "claimed". Add the counters to find the winner.

Another idea

Later on, you could make cards with spots grouped in different patterns to be matched with the spots on the page.

39

Win a prize

You will need: set of plastic numbers (you can use magnetic numbers)   paper bag   plastic or paper counters in two different colors

40

Learning notes

There is lots to look at in this number matching game. The activity will help your child to recognize numbers from 1-9.

To play the game

This is a game for two players.

Put the plastic numbers into a bag. The players take turns to pick out a number and see if they can match it to one on the picture. If they can, a counter is put on the object they have won. The numbers are returned to the bag. The game finishes when all the "prizes" have been won.

Collect the counters and count them up to see who has the most. You could also lay them in two rows according to their color and see who has the longest line.

41

Pie in the oven

 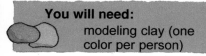

3 Go on 2

4

5

Bird pecks pie
Go back 3

13

14

2

6 Greedy cat
Go back to start

12

1

7

11

Start

Go on 2

8 Spilled milk
Go back 1

9

10

To make the pies

Roll a small piece of modeling clay into a ball and press it inside a bottle top. Place a tiny ball of clay on top.

Mark a pattern around the edge using the end of a plastic straw. Make a pie for each player using a different color.

Hints

•If you have only one color modeling clay, make different markings on the pies, or color them with some food coloring.

•Use large buttons if you don't want to make pies.

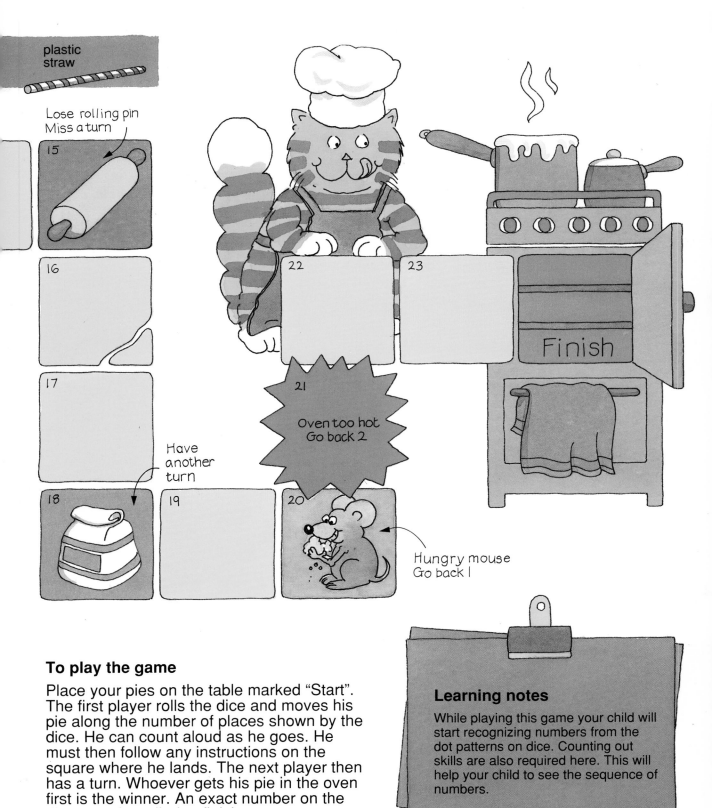

plastic straw

Lose rolling pin
Miss a turn

15

16

17

Have another turn

18

19

20 — Hungry mouse Go back 1

21 — Oven too hot Go back 2

22

23

Finish

To play the game

Place your pies on the table marked "Start". The first player rolls the dice and moves his pie along the number of places shown by the dice. He can count aloud as he goes. He must then follow any instructions on the square where he lands. The next player then has a turn. Whoever gets his pie in the oven first is the winner. An exact number on the dice must be rolled to finish.

Learning notes

While playing this game your child will start recognizing numbers from the dot patterns on dice. Counting out skills are also required here. This will help your child to see the sequence of numbers.

43

Cups and saucers

You will need:
 cardboard egg box
 stiff paper
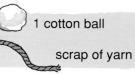 1 cotton ball
pencil
scrap of yarn
 rounded scissors
 ruler

To make the cups

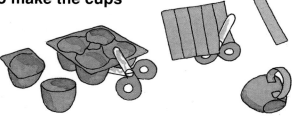

To make the mouse

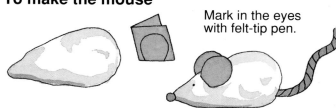

Mark in the eyes with felt-tip pen.

Cut the egg box into six separate sections and trim around each edge to make six cup shapes.

Cut six strips of stiff paper 5cm by 1cm (2in by ½in). Glue one end near the top of the cup and then bend the strip back and glue it at the base.

Pull off one third of a cotton ball and then tease it into a pear shape.

Cut out pink paper ears and glue them onto the head end. Stick on a tiny paper nose and a scrap of yarn for the tail.

1

2

3

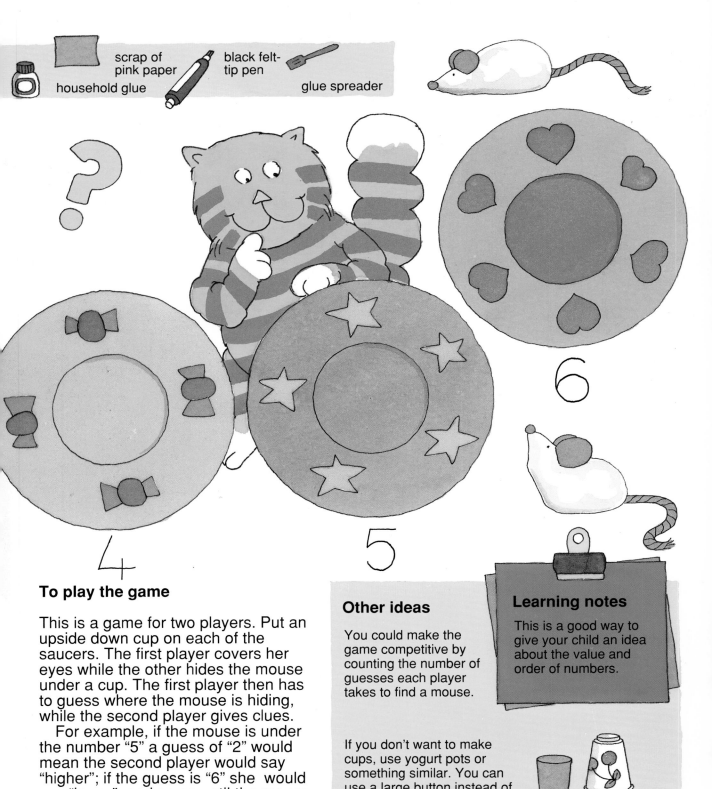

scrap of pink paper

household glue

black felt-tip pen

glue spreader

To play the game

This is a game for two players. Put an upside down cup on each of the saucers. The first player covers her eyes while the other hides the mouse under a cup. The first player then has to guess where the mouse is hiding, while the second player gives clues.

For example, if the mouse is under the number "5" a guess of "2" would mean the second player would say "higher"; if the guess is "6" she would say "lower", and so on until the mouse is found. Players take turns guessing and hiding.

Other ideas

You could make the game competitive by counting the number of guesses each player takes to find a mouse.

If you don't want to make cups, use yogurt pots or something similar. You can use a large button instead of a mouse.

Learning notes

This is a good way to give your child an idea about the value and order of numbers.

45

Build a house bingo

You will need:

thin red cardboard

ruler

pencil

set of plastic numbers

rounded scissors

paper bag

To make the bricks

6cm (2½in)

into 30 rectangles, each

Cut a piece of thin red cardboard to measure 30cm by 6cm (12in by 2½in). With a pencil, rule it into 30 rectangles, each 3cm wide and 2cm long (1¼in by ¾in). Cut them out to make bricks.

To play the game

This is a game for 2 players. Each player has 15 red bricks. Players choose which house on the double page they would like to build. Put the plastic numbers in the bag.

Players then take turns pulling a number out of the bag. (They mustn't look.) If a player picks a number which matches the number on a brick space on her house, she can cover the space with a red brick. The number is put back into the bag - give the bag a shake between turns. The first player to build her house (that is, cover the brick spaces) is the winner.

Spiders go home

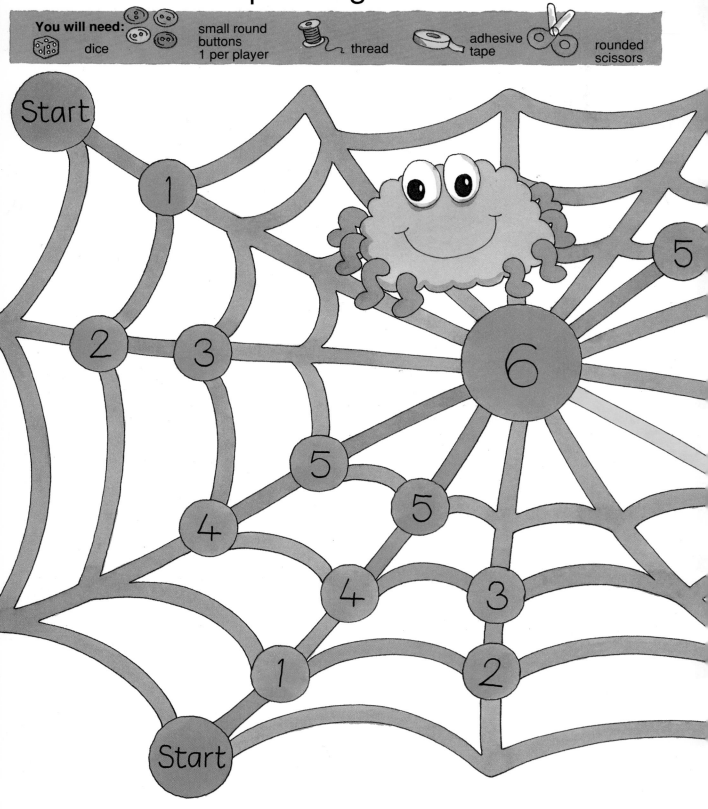

48

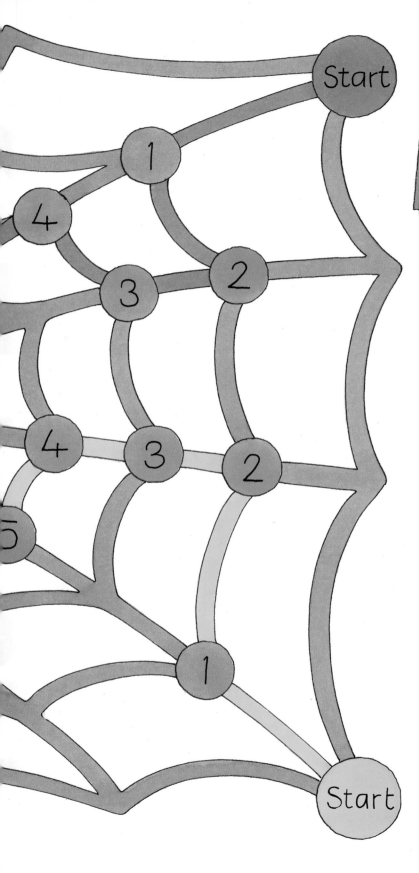

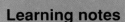

Learning notes

This game will help your child understand the ordering of numbers. As they move along a path by progressing from numbers one to six, children will begin to understand that numbers occur in a particular order.

To make the baby spiders

Cut a small piece of tape and then lay four lengths of thread on the sticky side. Now press on a small round button.

The holes in the buttons are the eyes.

Trim the legs so they are about 1cm (½in) each side. Make one spider for each player.

To play the game

This game is for two or three players.

Each player chooses a path on the spider's web and places a baby spider on a "Start" place. The players take turns throwing the dice. In order to move to the first position players must throw a "1". To move to the next place on the web they must throw a "2" and so on until a "6" is thrown and a baby spider reaches home. The first player to do this is the winner.

Once children get the idea of this game they can play it by themselves, racing one spider against another.

Teddy bear race

You will need:
One teddy bear per player

rounded scissors

dinner plate

old newspaper

To make a spinner

With a piece of chalk, draw around a dinner plate on some hard flat ground. If you are indoors, draw on a piece of cardboard.

Mark six sections on the circle, as shown. Number each section from 1-6. Put the plastic knife in the middle.

To make a path

Cut newspaper into rectangles that are large enough for teddies to sit on. Lay two winding paths across the floor or garden using an equal number of sheets - 15 or more.

chalk

plastic knife

If it is a windy day, weigh the paper down with stones.

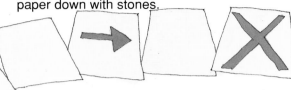

You can mark a large cross on the "start", and "finish" squares, and draw arrows along the path.

To play the game

This is a game for two players.

Players take turns to spin the knife and see which number the blade end points to. They then move their teddy that number of squares along their chosen path. The first teddy to reach the end of the path wins - an exact number must be spun in order to reach the end of the path.

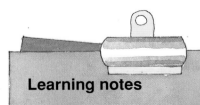

Learning notes

This active counting-out game will introduce such ordinal numbers as "first" and "second". Your child can eventually play this game himself, racing toys against each other.

Outdoor counting games

Throw and count

Players take turns throwing balls into a large cardboard box with a hole cut in its side. The balls can be made from rolled up socks. Players have six turns. Use a piece of string as a starting line. Count up the "hits" and "misses".

Find and count

Give each player a sheet of paper with numbers 1-6 written on it – space out the numbers well. Players look around the garden and collect objects to match the numbers on their sheet. They can find leaves, twigs, fallen petals and so on. Make sure they know that such objects as flower heads are not to be collected.

Spotting game

Set tasks for your child when out on a journey. Ask her to spot 2 horses, 10 red cars, 3 white trucks and so on.

New shoes

You will need: paper plate   ballpoint pen   wing paper fastener   pasta shells    ruler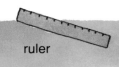

To make the spinner

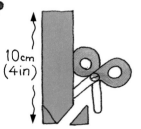

Turn over a large paper plate and on the back rule it into four sections. Number the sections as shown.

Cut a piece of thin cardboard into a strip 10cm by 2cm (4in by ¾in). Snip one end of the strip to make a point.

Poke a hole in the middle of the plate and in the pointer 1cm (½in) from its straight edge. Use a ballpoint pen to do this.

52

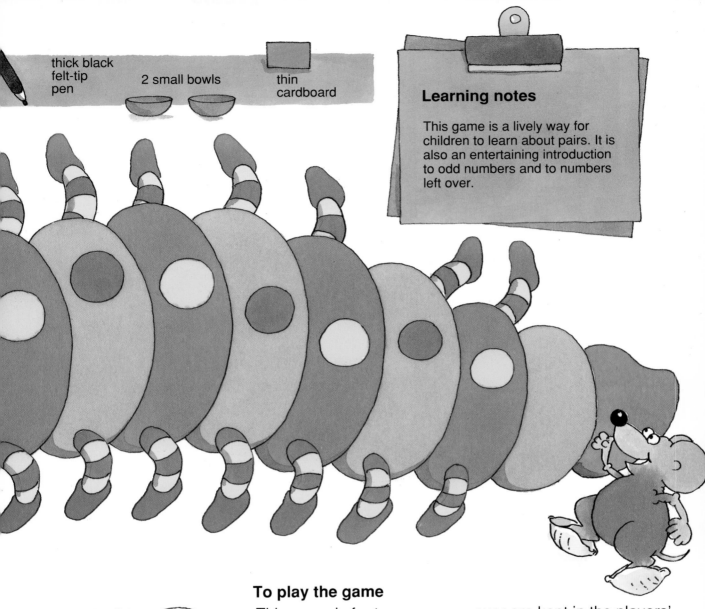

thick black felt-tip pen

2 small bowls

thin cardboard

Learning notes

This game is a lively way for children to learn about pairs. It is also an entertaining introduction to odd numbers and to numbers left over.

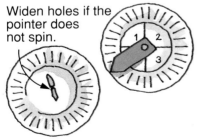

Widen holes if the pointer does not spin.

Push a paper fastener through the pointer and the middle of the plate, and then open its wings. Make sure the pointer spins smoothly.

To play the game

This game is for two players. The idea of the game is to fit on the caterpillar's new "pairs" of shoes.

Put a pile of pasta shells between the players, and give them a bowl each. Players take turns spinning the pointer. They then take the number of pasta shells shown by the pointer and place the "pasta" shoes, in pairs, on the caterpillar's feet. Any odd shoes left over are kept in the players' bowls to be counted later. For instance, a "4" turned up means two pairs of shoes can be fitted; a three will mean one pair plus an odd one left over.

When the caterpillar has all his shoes fitted, players count up the number of "odd" shoes they have each collected in their bowls. Whoever has the smallest number of "odd" shoes is the winner.

Jungle safari

You will need: thin white cardboard · thick black felt-tip pen · ruler · pencil · rounded scissors · paper in two different colours

To make the cards

| 1 | 2 | 3 | 4 |
| 5 | 6 | bush | raincloud |

Cut thin white cardboard into 8 pieces measuring 5cm by 4cm (3in by 1½in). Now number the cards, as shown, draw a bush on one of the remaining cards and a raincloud on the other.

To make the tents

←12½cm (7in)→ finished "tent"

Cut the paper into pieces measuring 12½cm by 6cm (7in by 2½in). Now draw ten rectangles on each piece measuring 3cm by 2½cm (1¼in by ¾in) and cut them out. Fold them by putting the short edges together, then open them slightly so they stand like tents.

To play the game

This is a game for two players. The object of the game is to see who can "spot" the most animals - to do this players have to set up their tents in the jungle.

Each player chooses a tent color. Shuffle the cards together and place them face down between the players. Players take turns picking up a card and reading the number. If the number on the card can be matched to a group of animals, for example, a "2" card is matched to two lions, then the lions are claimed by a player pitching his tent by them. If a number can't be matched a turn is missed.

If a bush is turned up, it means the animals are hiding and no tents can be placed. If a player picks a raincloud, one of his tents has been washed away and he must take it away.

When all the cards are used, they are re-shuffled and play begins again. The game is over when all the animals have a tent pitched by them. The winner has the most tents set up.

Learning notes

For young children, numbers can seem very abstract. This game which matches number symbols with groups of objects will help children visualize numbers and to understand their value.

Rabbit tails

You will need: household glue • glue spreader • pink and white cotton balls • stiff white paper • thin white cardboard • rounded scissors • felt-tip pens

To make the rabbit tails

Cut two pieces of stiff white paper 5cm by 4cm (2in by 1½in). Cover them with glue then spread and press a white cotton ball on one piece, and a pink cotton ball on the other.

Let the glue dry thoroughly. Now cut the pieces into small squares about 1cm by 1cm (½in by ½in). These are your rabbit tails.

To make the cards

Cut thin white cardboard into 12 pieces 5cm by 4cm (2in by 1½in). Draw large carrots on two of the cards; write "1" on four cards; "2" on three cards; "3" on two cards and "4" on the remaining one.

56

Learning notes

This game will give your child plenty of practice in recognizing and counting out numbers. It also introduces a very basic taking away exercise.

To play the game

This is a game for two players. Players choose pink or white tails. The cards are shuffled and placed face down in a pile. Players take turns picking up a card and, according to the number shown, putting tails on the rabbits. For instance, if a "3" card is turned up, three of the rabbits on the page can be given a tail.

` If a carrot card is turned up, two tails have to be taken away. The game is over when all the rabbits have tails - an exact number has to be turned up to finish. Take off the tails and lay them in two rows by color. The longest row is the winner.

Other ideas

Start with an equal number of tails on the page, and then take them off according to the number shown on the cards. A carrot card means you must put back two tails. The first one to remove all her tails is the winner.

For very young children, you could use this picture to play counting games. For example, see how many white rabbits there are, or how many are eating, jumping, hiding, have floppy ears and so on.

Cherry pie

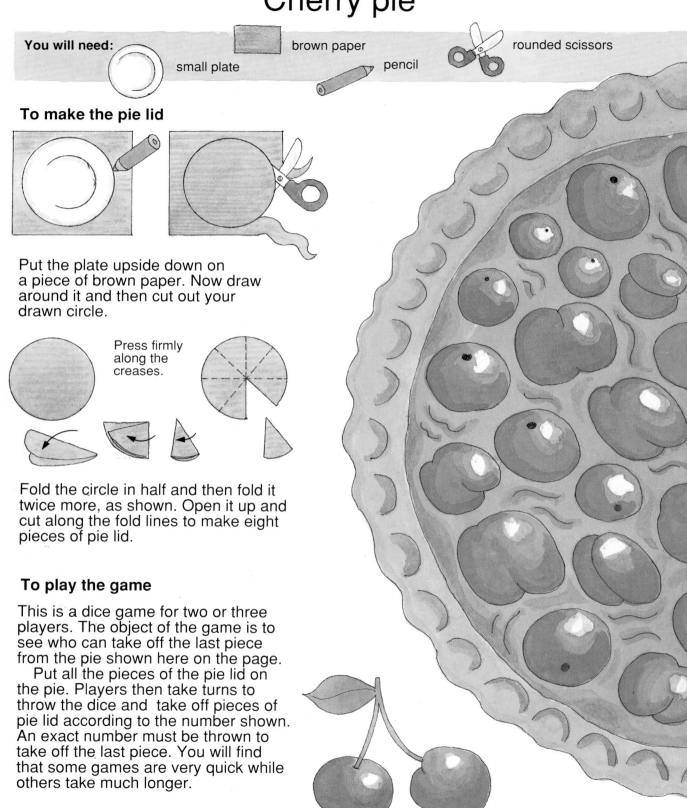

You will need:

small plate

brown paper

pencil

rounded scissors

To make the pie lid

Put the plate upside down on a piece of brown paper. Now draw around it and then cut out your drawn circle.

Press firmly along the creases.

Fold the circle in half and then fold it twice more, as shown. Open it up and cut along the fold lines to make eight pieces of pie lid.

To play the game

This is a dice game for two or three players. The object of the game is to see who can take off the last piece from the pie shown here on the page.
   Put all the pieces of the pie lid on the pie. Players then take turns to throw the dice and take off pieces of pie lid according to the number shown. An exact number must be thrown to take off the last piece. You will find that some games are very quick while others take much longer.

dice

Learning notes

This is a good game to start children predicting numbers. Try to encourage them to figure out what number they need to roll in order to win the game. The game also introduces the idea of "taking away" as pieces are removed and the rest are counted.

Other ideas

Players could keep a game score by collecting a "cherry stone" - a small prize - each time they win a game. After an agreed number of games, say, five, the "cherry stones" are counted up and whoever has the most is the winner.

Try playing this game the other way around and put the pieces on the pie according to the numbers on the dice.

Quack! Quack!

You will need: small ball of yarn · thick black felt-tip pen · rounded scissors · blue food coloring · orange felt-tip pen · 2 egg boxes · tape

To make the ponds

Trace this shape.

You will now see the shape appear on the white paper.

Trace the duck onto greaseproof paper, press hard with the pencil so you get a thick line.

Turn over your tracing and lay it on white paper. Go over the lines showing through, pressing hard with your pencil.

Cut out the duck shape, color the beak orange and mark in the eyes. Make two ducks.

5cm (2in)

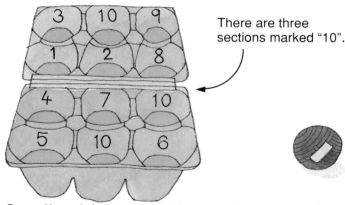

There are three sections marked "10".

Tape each duck onto the outside of a tumbler 5cm (2in) from the base. Pour a few drops of blue food coloring into the bottom of each "pond".

Cut off and throw away the tops of the egg boxes. Tape the bottom halves together. Number each section with black felt-tip pen, as shown.

Tape the end of your ball of yarn to stop it from unravelling. You could use a small rubber ball instead.

Hints

• Place the number box so that your child can aim and throw successfully.

• To save time you could cut out two greaseproof paper shapes and color them yellow.

• You can make this game quicker by using dessert spoons instead of teaspoons.

60

2 teaspoons

cold water

2 cereal bowls

pencil

ruler

2 clear plastic tumblers

white paper

greaseproof paper

To play the game

This game is for two players. Each player has a "pond" each, a bowl of water and a teaspoon. They take turns throwing the ball of yarn into a numbered section of the egg box. The number marked shows how many teaspoons of water a player can put into her glass. The first one to fill her tumbler to the level of the duck's bottom can shout "quack quack" and win the game. Wear waterproof overalls for this game.

Learning notes

This watery game will help your child to count up to ten. You can also use the opportunity to explain the meanings of words such as "more" and "less".

Park your cars

You will need:

thin white cardboard

ruler

rounded scissors

felt-tip pens

CARS

LIFT 10	LIFT 10
9	9
8	8
7	7
START 6	START 6
5	5

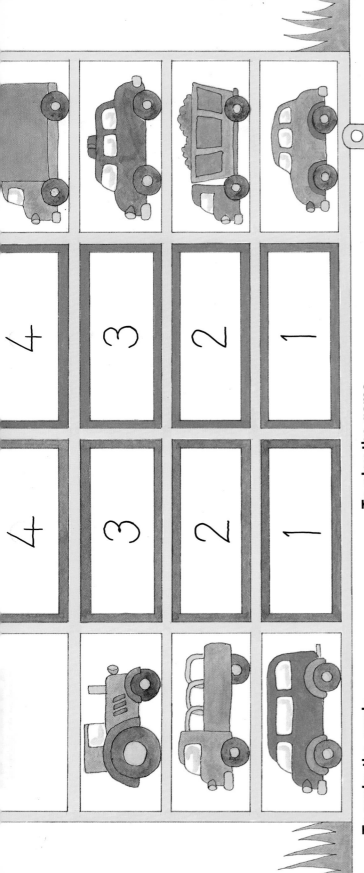

4	4
3	3
2	2
1	1

To make the cards

From thin white cardboard cut 12 cards measuring 5cm by 4cm (2in by 1½in). Mark the cards as shown (two of each).

| 1 up | 2 up | 3 up |
| 1 down | 2 down | 3 down |

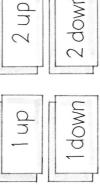   

Make four more cards to measure 4½cm by 2cm (1¾in by ¾in). Then draw a truck, a car, or a van on each of these smaller cards.

To play the game

This is a game for two players. Each has two "car" cards. Players choose the red or blue car lift. They then put one of their cars on "floor 6".

The large cards are shuffled and then placed face down in a pile. Players take turns picking a card and moving their vehicles up or down according to the instructions on the card. If a car lands next to an empty parking space it can be moved into that space, only then can a player put his second car on the "Start" position. If a card shows a greater number than there are spaces to move, the player has to miss a turn. The first person to park both his vehicles is the winner.

Learning notes

In this game, your child will be counting on and back along a line so introducing, in a very practical way, first elements of adding and subtracting.

Hint

You can use tiny toy cars instead of "car" cards.

Materials and equipment

Some of the games in this book involve making things as well as playing, and it can be fun for you and your child to cut, paint and glue together. You can store your game pieces in envelopes and cover any cards with sticky-backed plastic for safe-keeping.

The specific things you need for each project are listed at the top of each page. Below is some general advice on materials and equipment.

Plastic numbers are often magnetic and can be bought in educational toy stores. You can always use small cards with numbers written on if you don't own a set.

Scissors should be rounded . If you use sharp scissors don't forget to put them away after use. Try and draw clear outlines for your child to cut. If you are cutting out cards or paper "bricks", it is a good idea to cut long strips and then let your child cut them up into smaller separate pieces.

Felt-tip pens should be nontoxic and washable. Use thick or thin ones depending on the size of paper you are using. Black numbers written on white is very clear and easily understood.

Glue: household glue is a safe glue for your child to use. You can buy it in large stationery stores or educational toy stores. It is washable, but it is a good idea to wipe up spills as soon as possible and to wear aprons or overalls. If it is spilled on clothes, soak them in cold water to make sure there is no staining. This glue can also be used as a paint thickener or varnish: it is white but is clear when dry. Glue sticks are good for using on small areas.

When gluing small pieces, such as wool tails on mice, it is a good idea to pour a little glue into an old saucer and lightly dip in the pieces rather than use a glue brush.

Thin cardboard can be bought in art supply stores and stationery stores. Stiff, thick paper is a good alternative, but make sure that the numbers can't be seen when the cards are face down.

Colored papers can be saved from used packaging. Unused wallpapers will give you different colors and patterns when you need a contrast. You can also color stiff white paper with paint mixed with a little household glue.

Paints should be water-based and nontoxic. Mix or thin colors on old plates, and use mugs for water as they are safer than glass containers.

Modeling clay is available from toy and stationary stores. You can also use a little uncooked pastry dyed with a little food coloring, or mix flour, salt and water to a clay texture.

Bags: it is a good idea, when using bags for a game, to remind children never to put any kind of bag over their heads.